ESCAPE THE RAT RACE

Learn How Money Works
and Become a Rich Kid

Robert Kiyosaki

Author of bestseller *Rich Dad Poor Dad*

Published by Plata Publishing, LLC

CASHFLOW, Rich Dad, and Rich Kid Smart Kid are registered trademarks of CASHFLOW Technologies, Inc.

 is a registered trademark of CASHFLOW Technologies, Inc.

Plata Publishing, LLC
4330 N. Civic Center Plaza
Suite 100
Scottsdale, AZ 85251
(480) 998-6971

Visit our websites: PlataPublishing.com and RichDad.com

Printed in the United States of America
First Edition: January 2005
First Plata Publishing Edition: November 2012
ISBN: 978-1-61268-055-2

CREATIVE CREDITS:	Rantz Hoseley	Writer & Inks	Cory Nelson	Writer
	Ben Plouffe	Penciler, Colorist	James Offredi	Colorist
	Michael Yamada	Penciler	Blambot's NatePiekos	Letterer

Best-Selling Books and Games by Robert T. Kiyosaki

BOOKS

Rich Dad Poor Dad
**What the Rich Teach Their Kids About Money –
That the Poor and Middle Class Do Not**

Rich Dad's CASHFLOW Quadrant
Guide to Financial Freedom

Rich Dad's Guide to Investing
What the Rich Invest In That the Poor and Middle Class Do Not

Rich Dad's Rich Kid Smart Kid
Give Your Child a Financial Head Start

Rich Dad's Retire Young Retire Rich
How to Get Rich and Stay Rich

Rich Dad's Prophecy
**Why the Biggest Stock Market Crash in History Is Still Coming...
And How You Can Prepare Yourself and Profit from It!**

Rich Dad's Success Stories
**Real-Life Success Stories from Real-Life People
Who Followed the Rich Dad Lessons**

*Rich Dad's Guide to Becoming Rich
Without Cutting Up Your Credit Cards*
Turn Bad Debt into Good Debt

Rich Dad's Who Took My Money?
Why Slow Investors Lose and Fast Money Wins!

Rich Dad Poor Dad for Teens
The Secrets About Money – That You Don't Learn in School!

Rich Dad's Escape the Rat Race
Learn How Money Works and Become a Rich Kid

Rich Dad's Before You Quit Your Job
Ten Real-Life Lessons Every Entrepreneur Should Know
About Building a Multimillion-Dollar Business

Rich Dad's Increase Your Financial IQ
Get Smarter with Your Money

Conspiracy of the Rich
The 8 New Rules of Money

Unfair Advantage
The Power of Financial Education

GAMES

CASHFLOW® for Kids

CASHFLOW® 101

CASHFLOW® 202

1

Meet Tina, Tim and Red

3

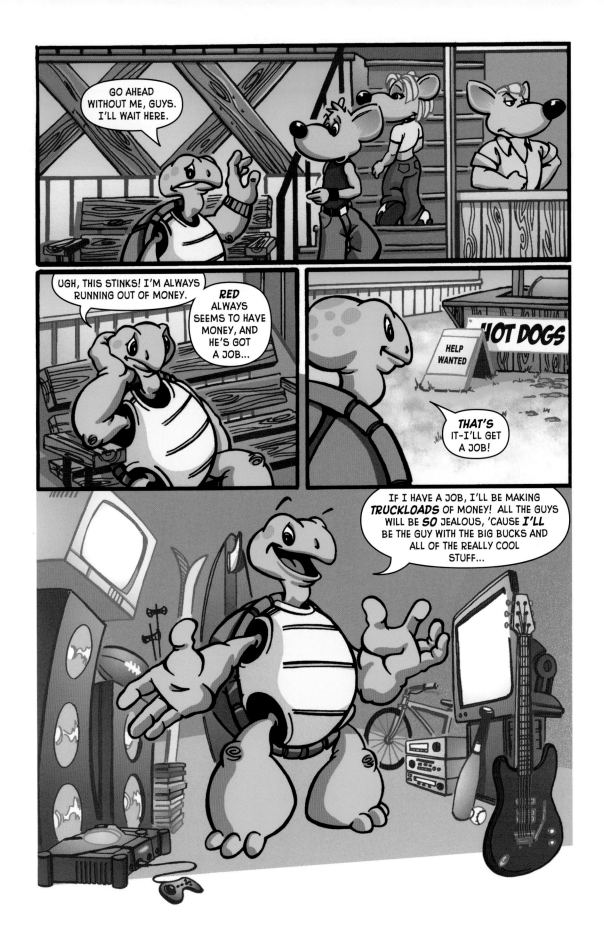

6

8

9

10

2

Robert's Story

ROBERT'S DAD WAS A TEACHER. BUT EVEN THOUGH HE WAS REALLY SMART AND HAD A GOOD JOB, HE DIDN'T HAVE MUCH MONEY.

WELL, SON, IF YOU WANT TO BE RICH, YOU HAVE TO LEARN TO MAKE MONEY.

BUT... HOW DO I MAKE MONEY?

WELL, USE YOUR HEAD, SON.

WHICH REALLY MEANT, "THAT'S ALL I'M GOING TO TELL YOU," OR "I DON'T KNOW THE ANSWER, SO DON'T EMBARRASS ME."

SO THAT SATURDAY MORNING, MIKE BECAME HIS FIRST BUSINESS PARTNER.

THE NEXT MORNING, ROBERT TOLD HIS BEST FRIEND, MIKE, WHAT HIS DAD HAD SAID. THEY CAME UP WITH A PLAN.

MIKE HAD GOTTEN AN INSPIRATION FROM A BOOK HE HAD READ, SO THEY STARTED A BUSINESS. FOR THE NEXT SEVERAL WEEKS, MIKE AND ROBERT RAN AROUND THEIR NEIGHBORHOOD, KNOCKING ON DOORS...

... ASKING THEIR NEIGHBORS IF THEY COULD HAVE THEIR USED TOOTHPASTE TUBES.

SOME ASKED WHAT THEY WERE DOING, BUT ROBERT AND MIKE JUST SAID, "WE CAN'T TELL YOU. IT'S A BUSINESS SECRET."

14

WHEN THEY HAD ENOUGH TUBES, THEY STARTED PRODUCTION.

THE ASSEMBLY LINE WAS CREATED IN ROBERT'S DRIVEWAY.

ROBERT'S DAD AND A FRIEND OF HIS SHOWED UP TO FIND THE PRODUCTION IN FULL SWING.

SEE, BACK IN 1956 TOOTHPASTE DIDN'T COME IN PLASTIC TUBES...

IT CAME IN LEAD TUBES. MELTING THE *LEAD* TUBES WAS THE KEY TO ROBERT AND MIKE'S IDEA OF HOW TO MAKE THEM *RICH*.

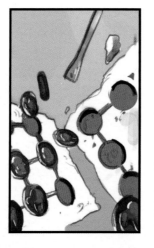

I GUESS JIMMY AND HIS FRIENDS ARE RIGHT. WE *ARE* POOR.

BOYS, YOU'RE ONLY POOR IF YOU GIVE UP. THE MOST IMPORTANT THING IS THAT YOU DID SOMETHING. MOST PEOPLE ONLY TALK AND DREAM OF GETTING RICH. YOU'VE DONE SOMETHING.

I'M VERY PROUD OF THE TWO OF YOU. KEEP GOING. DON'T QUIT.

SO HOW COME YOU'RE NOT RICH, DAD?

BECAUSE I CHOSE TO BE A SCHOOLTEACHER. SCHOOL-TEACHERS REALLY DON'T THINK ABOUT BEING RICH. WE JUST LIKE TO TEACH. IF YOU BOYS WANT TO LEARN HOW TO BE RICH, TALK TO *YOUR* DAD, MIKE.

MY DAD?

YEAH, YOUR DAD AND I HAVE THE SAME BANKER, AND HE RAVES ABOUT YOUR FATHER.

HE TELLS ME THAT YOUR FATHER IS BRILLIANT WHEN IT COMES TO MAKING MONEY.

THEN HOW COME WE DON'T HAVE A NICE CAR AND A NICE HOUSE LIKE THE RICH KIDS AT SCHOOL?

HAVING A NICE CAR AND A NICE HOUSE DOESN'T MEAN YOU'RE RICH OR THAT YOU KNOW HOW TO MAKE MONEY.

17

JIMMY'S DAD WORKS FOR THE SUGAR PLANTATION. HE'S NOT MUCH DIFFERENT FROM ME. HE WORKS FOR A COMPANY, AND I WORK FOR THE GOVERNMENT. THE COMPANY BUYS THE CAR FOR HIM. BUT THE SUGAR COMPANY IS IN FINANCIAL TROUBLE, AND JIMMY'S DAD MAY SOON HAVE NOTHING.

YOUR DAD IS DIFFERENT, MIKE. HE SEEMS TO BE BUILDING AN EMPIRE, AND I SUSPECT IN A FEW YEARS HE WILL BE A VERY RICH MAN.

THE THINGS ROBERT'S DAD HAD SAID GOT MIKE AND ROBERT EXCITED AGAIN. AS THEY CLEANED THE MESS, THEY MADE PLANS TO TALK TO MIKE'S DAD THE NEXT SATURDAY.

SO, AT 7:30 ON SATURDAY MORNING, ROBERT CAUGHT THE BUS TO THE POOR SIDE OF TOWN.

C'MON, FOLLOW ME.

18

19

OK, HERE'S MY OFFER. I'LL TEACH YOU, BUT I WON'T DO IT CLASSROOM-STYLE. YOU WORK FOR ME, I'LL TEACH YOU. YOU DON'T WORK FOR ME, I WON'T TEACH YOU.

I CAN TEACH YOU FASTER IF YOU WORK, AND I'M WASTING MY TIME IF YOU JUST WANT TO SIT AND LISTEN LIKE YOU DO IN SCHOOL. THAT'S MY OFFER. TAKE IT OR LEAVE IT.

TAKE IT.

TAKE IT.

GOOD. MRS. MARTIN WILL BE BY IN TEN MINUTES. AFTER I'M THROUGH WITH HER, YOU CAN RIDE WITH HER TO MY SUPERETTE AND START WORKING.

I'LL PAY YOU 10 CENTS AN HOUR AND YOU'LL WORK FOR THREE HOURS EVERY SATURDAY.

BUT I HAVE A SOFTBALL GAME TODAY.

TAKE IT...

...OR LEAVE IT.

I'LL TAKE IT.

PASSING UP SOFTBALL WAS TOUGH FOR ROBERT.

BUT HE KNEW THAT IF IT MEANT HE COULD BE RICH SOMEDAY, IT'D BE WORTH IT.

THE NEXT SATURDAY MORNING, MIKE AND ROBERT WERE WORKING FOR MRS. MARTIN.

SHE WAS A NICE WOMAN AND SAID THAT MIKE AND ROBERT REMINDED HER OF HER TWO SONS WHO HAD GROWN UP.

SHE WAS A TASK MASTER, THOUGH. THEY SPENT THREE HOURS TAKING CANS OFF THE SHELVES AND BRUSHING EACH CAN TO GET THE DUST OFF. THEN THEY HAD TO RE-STACK THEM NEATLY.

IT WAS EXCRUCIATING, *BORING* WORK.

MIKE'S DAD OWNED NINE OF THESE LITTLE SUPERETTES. THEY WERE LITTLE NEIGHBORHOOD GROCERY STORES WHERE PEOPLE BOUGHT STUFF LIKE MILK AND BREAD.

THE PROBLEM WAS, THIS WAS HAWAII--AND IN THE DAYS BEFORE AIR CONDITIONING, STORES COULD NOT CLOSE THEIR DOORS BECAUSE OF THE HEAT.

EVERY TIME A CAR DROVE BY, DUST WOULD SWIRL AND SETTLE IN THE STORE.

SO THEY HAD A JOB AS LONG AS THERE WAS NO AIR CONDITIONING.

FOR THREE WEEKS, MIKE AND ROBERT WORKED FOR THREE HOURS EACH SATURDAY. BY NOON, WORK WAS OVER, AND MRS. MARTIN DROPPED THREE DIMES IN EACH OF THEIR HANDS.

NOW, EVEN AT THE AGE OF NINE IN THE MID-1950S, 30 CENTS WASN'T TOO EXCITING. COMIC BOOKS COST 10 CENTS BACK THEN, SO ROBERT USUALLY SPENT HIS MONEY ON COMIC BOOKS AND WENT HOME.

FOUR WEEKS LATER, ROBERT WAS READY TO QUIT. HE HAD AGREED TO WORK ONLY BECAUSE HE WANTED TO LEARN TO MAKE MONEY FROM MIKE'S DAD, AND NOW HE FELT LIKE A SLAVE.

ON TOP OF THAT, HE HADN'T SEEN MIKE'S DAD SINCE THAT FIRST SATURDAY.

I'M QUITTING! SCHOOL IS BORING AND NOW I DON'T EVEN HAVE SATURDAYS TO LOOK FORWARD TO.

AND ALL FOR 30 LOUSY CENTS!

WHAT? WHAT IS IT?

DAD SAID THIS WOULD HAPPEN. HE SAID TO MEET WITH HIM WHEN YOU WERE READY TO QUIT.

WHAT?! HE'S BEEN WAITING FOR ME TO GET FED UP?

SORT OF. DAD'S KIND OF DIFFERENT. HE TEACHES DIFFERENTLY FROM YOUR DAD. YOUR MOM AND DAD LECTURE A LOT.

JUST WAIT TILL THIS SATURDAY. I'LL TELL HIM YOU'RE READY.

YOU MEAN I'VE BEEN SET UP?

NO, NOT REALLY, BUT... MAYBE. ANYWAY, DAD WILL EXPLAIN ON SATURDAY.

3

Robert Escapes the Trap

Tim

SO, AT EIGHT O'CLOCK THAT SATURDAY MORNING, ROBERT FOUND HIMSELF AT MIKE'S HOUSE AGAIN.

TAKE A SEAT AND WAIT IN LINE.

ROBERT FELT AWKWARD WAITING TO TALK TO MIKE'S DAD, BUT HE WAS DETERMINED TO GET WHAT HE DESERVED, SO HE SAT DOWN AND WAITED.

WAITED 20 MINUTES AS THE OLDER MAN SITTING NEXT TO HIM WENT IN TO TALK TO MIKE'S DAD...

WAITED 40 MINUTES AS THE NICE LADY WHO HAD OFFERED HIM A SEAT WENT IN TO TALK TO MIKE'S DAD...

WAITED UNTIL HE WAS STEAMING MAD-- AND THE ONLY PERSON STILL WAITING.

ROBERT COULD HEAR MIKE'S DAD TALKING ON THE PHONE, RUSTLING PAPERS...

...IGNORING HIM.

FINALLY, AT EXACTLY NINE O'CLOCK, MIKE'S DAD CAME OUT, SAID NOTHING, AND SIGNALED FOR ROBERT TO ENTER HIS OFFICE.

I UNDERSTAND YOU WANT A RAISE, OR YOU'RE GOING TO QUIT.

WELL, YOU'RE NOT KEEPING YOUR END OF THE BARGAIN! YOU SAID THAT YOU WOULD TEACH ME IF I WORKED FOR YOU. WELL, I'VE WORKED FOR YOU.

I'VE WORKED HARD. I'VE GIVEN UP MY SOFTBALL GAMES TO WORK FOR YOU AND YOU DON'T KEEP YOUR WORD.

YOU HAVEN'T TAUGHT ME *ANYTHING*. YOU'RE A *CROOK* LIKE EVERYONE IN TOWN THINKS YOU ARE.

YOU'RE GREEDY. YOU WANT ALL THE MONEY AND DON'T TAKE CARE OF YOUR EMPLOYEES. YOU MAKE ME WAIT AND DON'T SHOW ME ANY RESPECT.

I'M ONLY A LITTLE BOY, AND I DESERVE TO BE TREATED BETTER.

NOT BAD... IN LESS THAN A MONTH, YOU SOUND LIKE MOST OF MY EMPLOYEES.

WHAT?! I THOUGHT YOU WERE GOING TO KEEP YOUR END OF THE BARGAIN AND TEACH ME.

I AM TEACHING YOU.

27

I *HAVE* KEPT MY PROMISE. I'VE BEEN TEACHING YOU FROM AFAR. AT NINE YEARS OLD, YOU'VE GOTTEN A TASTE OF WHAT IT FEELS LIKE TO WORK FOR MONEY. JUST MULTIPLY YOUR LAST MONTH BY FIFTY YEARS AND YOU'LL HAVE AN IDEA OF WHAT MOST PEOPLE SPEND THEIR LIVES DOING.

HOW DID YOU FEEL WAITING IN LINE TO SEE ME?

TERRIBLE.

AND HOW DID YOU FEEL WHEN MRS. MARTIN DROPPED THREE DIMES IN YOUR HAND FOR THREE HOURS WORK?

I FELT LIKE IT WASN'T ENOUGH. IT SEEMED LIKE NOTHING. I WAS DISAPPOINTED.

THAT'S HOW MOST EMPLOYEES FEEL WHEN THEY LOOK AT THEIR PAYCHECKS. ESPECIALLY AFTER ALL THE TAX AND OTHER DEDUCTIONS ARE TAKEN OUT. AT LEAST YOU GOT 100%.

YOU MEAN MOST WORKERS DON'T GET PAID EVERYTHING?

HEAVENS, NO! THE GOVERNMENT TAKES ITS SHARE FIRST. YOU'RE TAXED WHEN YOU EARN. YOU'RE TAXED WHEN YOU SPEND. YOU'RE TAXED WHEN YOU SAVE. YOU'RE TAXED WHEN YOU DIE.

AS I SAID, THERE'S A *LOT* TO LEARN. LEARNING HOW TO HAVE MONEY WORK FOR *YOU* IS A LIFETIME STUDY.

29

SO, DO YOU STILL HAVE THE PASSION TO LEARN?

YOU BET!

GOOD. NOW GET BACK TO WORK. THIS TIME, I WILL PAY YOU NOTHING.

WHAT?!

YOU HEARD ME. *NOTHING.* YOU'LL WORK THE SAME THREE HOURS EVERY SATURDAY, BUT THIS TIME YOU WON'T BE PAID 10 CENTS PER HOUR.

YOU SAID YOU WANTED TO LEARN NOT TO WORK FOR MONEY, SO I'M NOT GOING TO PAY YOU ANYTHING.

THAT'S NOT FAIR! YOU'VE GOT TO PAY *SOME*THING.

I'VE ALREADY HAD THIS CONVERSATION WITH MIKE. HE'S ALREADY WORKING, DUSTING AND STACKING CANNED GOODS FOR FREE.

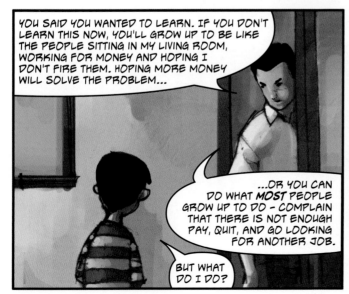

YOU SAID YOU WANTED TO LEARN. IF YOU DON'T LEARN THIS NOW, YOU'LL GROW UP TO BE LIKE THE PEOPLE SITTING IN MY LIVING ROOM, WORKING FOR MONEY AND HOPING I DON'T FIRE THEM. HOPING MORE MONEY WILL SOLVE THE PROBLEM...

...OR YOU CAN DO WHAT *MOST* PEOPLE GROW UP TO DO - COMPLAIN THAT THERE IS NOT ENOUGH PAY, QUIT, AND GO LOOKING FOR ANOTHER JOB.

BUT WHAT DO I DO?

USE YOUR HEAD. IF YOU USE IT WELL, YOU'LL SOON THANK ME FOR GIVING YOU AN OPPORTUNITY, AND YOU'LL GROW INTO A RICH MAN.

NOW, GET OUT OF HERE AND GET BACK TO WORK.

FOR THREE MORE WEEKS, MIKE AND ROBERT WORKED FOR THREE HOURS, EVERY SATURDAY, FOR NOTHING. ROBERT DIDN'T TELL HIS DAD HE WASN'T BEING PAID. HE WOULDN'T HAVE UNDERSTOOD.

OVER TIME, THE WORK ROUTINE GOT EASIER. BUT THEY WERE STILL SAD TO BE MISSING SOFTBALL GAMES AND NOT BEING ABLE TO AFFORD A FEW COMIC BOOKS.

THREE WEEKS LATER, MIKE'S DAD MET THEM AT THE STORE.

HOW'S IT GOING, BOYS?

OK...

YEAH, OK.

LEARN ANYTHING YET?

WELL, YOU BOYS HAD BETTER START THINKING. YOU'RE STARING AT ONE OF LIFE'S BIGGEST LESSONS.

LET'S GO FOR A WALK.

IF YOU LEARN THE LESSON, YOU'LL ENJOY A LIFE OF GREAT FREEDOM AND SECURITY. IF YOU DON'T LEARN THE LESSON, YOU'LL WIND UP LIKE MRS. MARTIN AND MOST OF THE PEOPLE PLAYING SOFTBALL IN THIS PARK.

THEY WORK VERY HARD, FOR LITTLE MONEY, CLINGING TO THE ILLUSION OF JOB SECURITY, LOOKING FORWARD TO A TWO TO THREE-WEEK VACATION EACH YEAR AND A SKIMPY PENSION AFTER FORTY-FIVE YEARS OF WORK.

IF THAT EXCITES YOU, I'LL GIVE YOU A RAISE TO 25 CENTS AN HOUR.

DOESN'T THAT 25 CENTS AN HOUR SOUND GOOD? DOESN'T IT MAKE YOUR HEART BEAT A LITTLE FASTER?

NO.

BUT IT **WAS** TEMPTING TO ROBERT. AT THE TIME, 25 CENTS WAS BIG BUCKS.

OK, HOW ABOUT IF I PAY YOU A DOLLAR, THEN.

NO.

BUT ROBERT'S BRAIN WAS SCREAMING; *"TAKE IT, TAKE IT!"*

OK, $2 AN HOUR.

IN 1956, GETTING PAID $2 AN HOUR WOULD HAVE MADE ROBERT THE RICHEST KID IN THE WORLD.

HE COULD SEE IN HIS MIND ALL THE THINGS THAT KIND OF MONEY COULD GET HIM. A NEW BIKE, A NEW BASEBALL GLOVE, STACKS OF COMICS.

BUT **SOMEHOW** HE MANAGED TO KEEP HIS MOUTH SHUT.

OK, $5 AN HOUR.

32

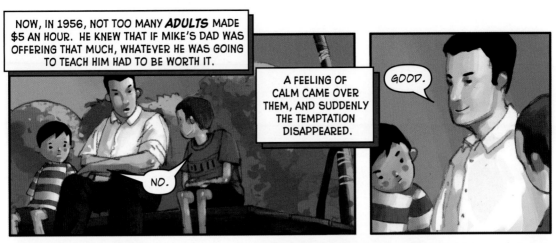

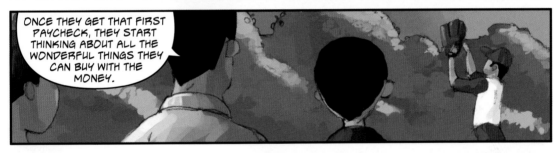

33

IT'S LIKE A DONKEY, DRAGGING A CART, WITH ITS OWNER DANGLING A CARROT JUST IN FRONT OF ITS NOSE.

THE DONKEY'S OWNER MAY BE GOING WHERE HE WANTS TO GO, BUT THE DONKEY IS CHASING AN ILLUSION. TOMORROW THERE WILL ONLY BE ANOTHER CARROT FOR THE DONKEY.

YOU MEAN THE MOMENT I BEGAN TO PICTURE A NEW BASEBALL GLOVE, CANDY, AND TOYS, THAT'S LIKE A CARROT TO A DONKEY?

EXACTLY. AND AS YOU GET OLDER, YOUR TOYS GET MORE EXPENSIVE. A NEW CAR, A BOAT, AND A BIG HOUSE TO IMPRESS YOUR FRIENDS. *THAT'S* THE TRAP.

SO, WHAT'S THE ANSWER?

YOU NEED TO OPEN YOUR MIND AND START LOOKING FOR OPPORTUNITIES.

TO LIVE A LIFE DICTATED BY THE SIZE OF A PAYCHECK IS NOT REALLY A LIFE. THINKING THAT A JOB WILL MAKE YOU FEEL SECURE IS LYING TO YOURSELF.

KEEP USING YOUR BRAIN, AND SOON YOU'LL SEE THINGS THAT OTHER PEOPLE NEVER SEE. OPPORTUNITIES RIGHT IN FRONT OF THEIR NOSES.

THE MOMENT YOU SEE ONE OPPORTUNITY, YOU'LL SEE THEM FOR THE REST OF YOUR LIFE.

34

FOR TWO MORE WEEKS ROBERT AND MIKE KEPT THINKING, TALKING, AND WORKING FOR FREE.

AT THE END OF THE SECOND SATURDAY, ROBERT SAW MRS. MARTIN CUTTING THE FRONT PAGE OF THE COMIC BOOKS IN HALF. ROBERT ASKED HER WHAT SHE WAS DOING.

I GIVE THE TOP HALF OF THE COVER BACK TO THE COMIC-BOOK DISTRIBUTOR FOR CREDIT WHEN HE BRINGS IN THE NEW COMICS AND I THROW THE REST OF THE BOOK AWAY.

HE'S COMING IN AN HOUR.

WHEN THE DISTRIBUTOR ARRIVED, ROBERT ASKED HIM IF THEY COULD KEEP THE COMIC BOOKS.

YOU CAN HAVE THEM IF YOU KEEP WORKING FOR THIS STORE AND DON'T SELL THEM.

AFTER CLEANING OUT THE BASEMENT AT MIKE'S HOUSE THE COMIC BOOK LIBRARY, WAS READY TO OPEN.

THEY CHARGED EACH CHILD 10 CENTS ADMISSION TO THE LIBRARY, WHICH WAS OPEN FOR TWO HOURS EVERY DAY AFTER SCHOOL.

THE CUSTOMERS WOULD READ AS MANY COMICS AS THEY COULD IN TWO HOURS.

IT WAS A BARGAIN FOR THEM, SINCE A COMIC COST 10 CENTS EACH, AND THEY COULD READ FIVE OR SIX IN TWO HOURS.

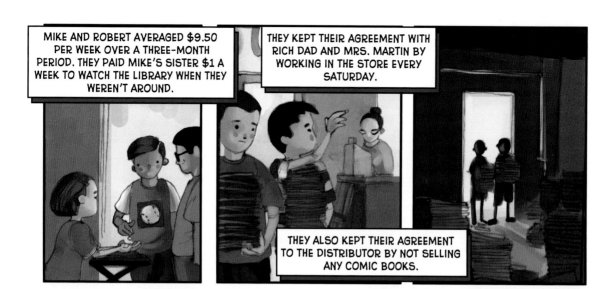

MIKE AND ROBERT AVERAGED $9.50 PER WEEK OVER A THREE-MONTH PERIOD. THEY PAID MIKE'S SISTER $1 A WEEK TO WATCH THE LIBRARY WHEN THEY WEREN'T AROUND.

THEY KEPT THEIR AGREEMENT WITH RICH DAD AND MRS. MARTIN BY WORKING IN THE STORE EVERY SATURDAY.

THEY ALSO KEPT THEIR AGREEMENT TO THE DISTRIBUTOR BY NOT SELLING ANY COMIC BOOKS.

MIKE'S DAD WAS EXCITED BECAUSE THEY HAD LEARNED THE FIRST LESSON SO WELL. HE HAD NEW THINGS HE COULD BEGIN TO TEACH THEM NOW.

BY NOT GETTING PAID TO WORK AT THE STORE, THEY WERE FORCED TO USE THEIR IMAGINATIONS TO SPOT AN OPPORTUNITY TO MAKE MONEY. BY STARTING THEIR OWN BUSINESS, THEY HAD TAKEN CONTROL OF THEIR OWN FINANCES, AND WERE NO LONGER DEPENDENT ON AN EMPLOYER.

INSTEAD OF PAYING THEM MONEY, MIKE'S DAD HAD GIVEN THEM MUCH MORE.

4

Opportunities Are Everywhere

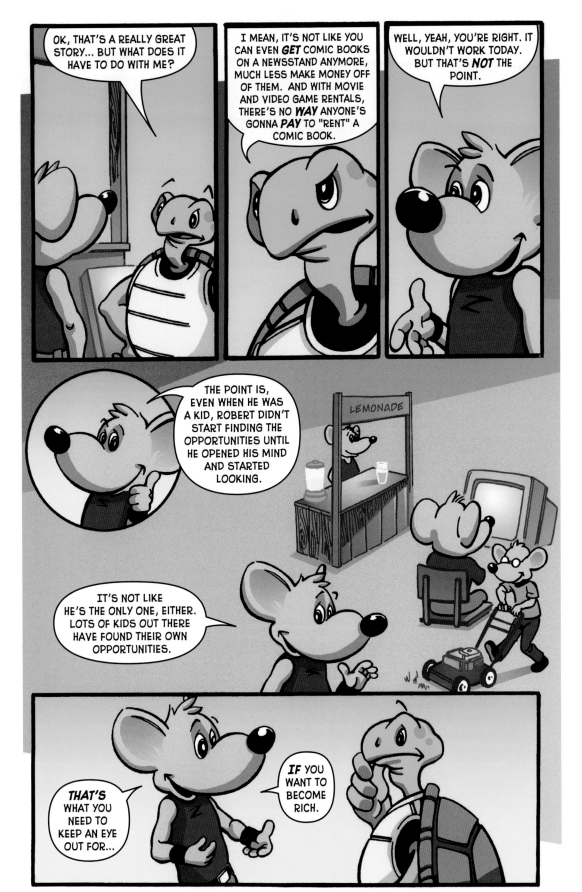

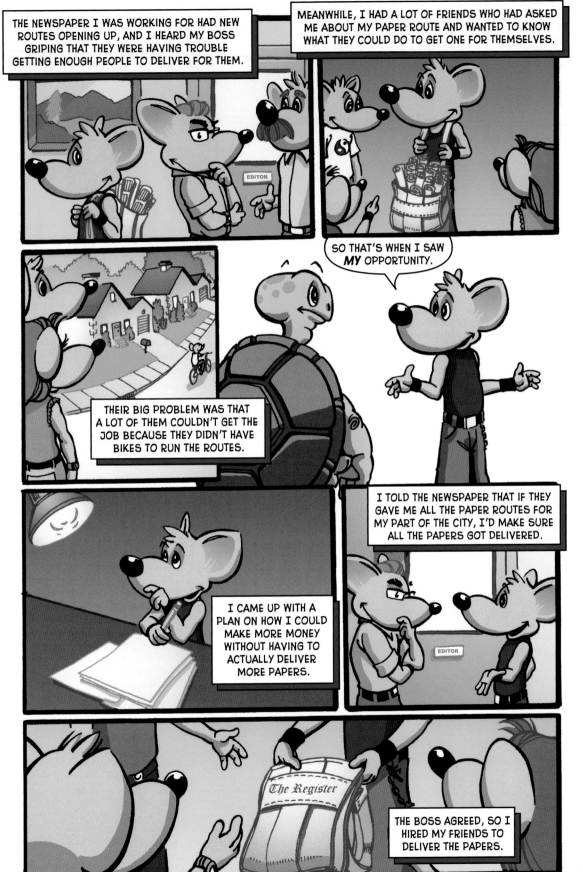

41

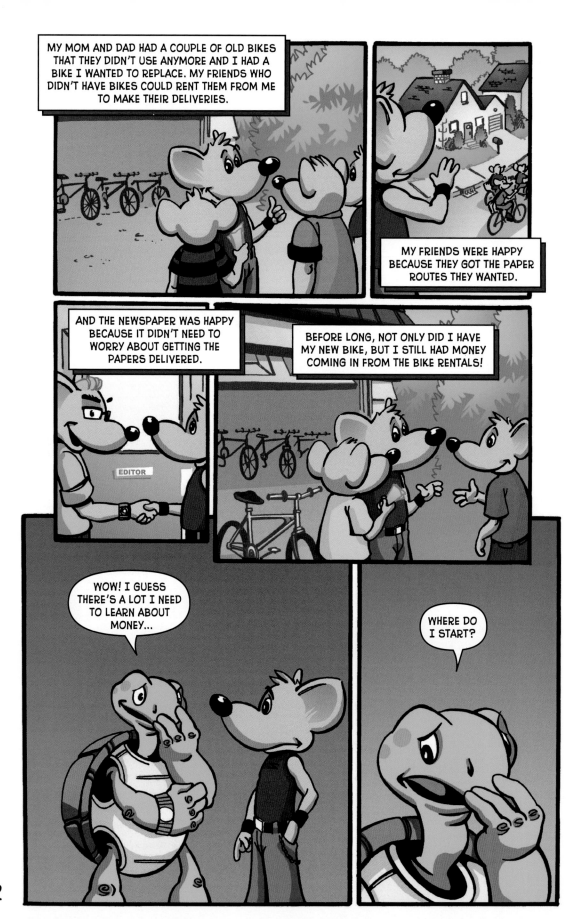

43

44

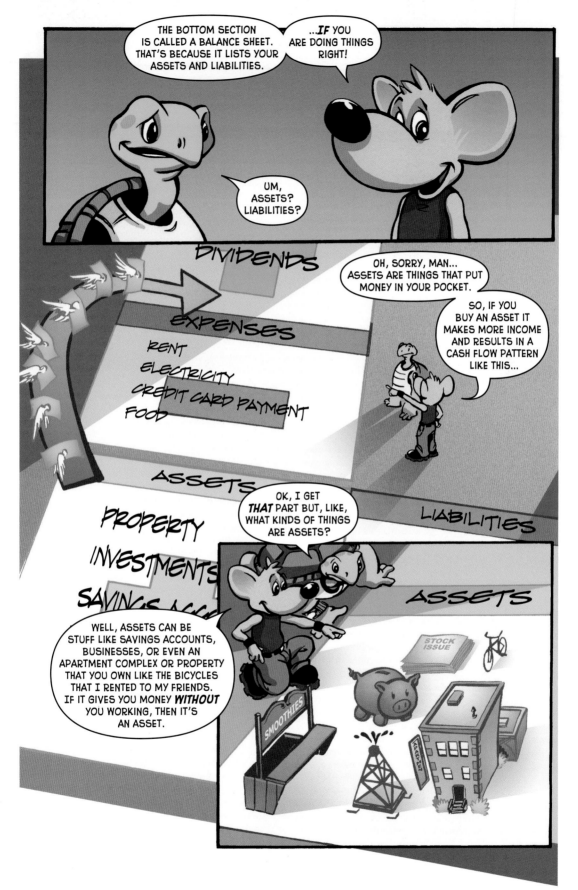

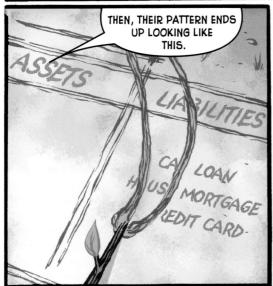

48

49

THEY WORK LIKE CRAZY BECAUSE THEY KNOW IF THEY DON'T PAY THEIR BILLS, THEY'LL LOSE ALL THE EXPENSIVE STUFF THEY'VE BOUGHT.

SO WHEN THEY ACTUALLY *CAN* SAVE UP SOME EXTRA MONEY, THEY'RE FREAKED OUT ABOUT DOING ANYTHING WITH IT. THEY'RE SCARED THEY MIGHT LOSE THEIR JOBS AND THAT MEANS THEY CAN'T PAY THOSE BILLS...

SO THEY GET STUCK IN THAT TRAP: SCARED TO DEATH, WORKING LIKE CRAZY, AND NEVER GETTING AHEAD. THAT'S CALLED THE RAT RACE.

NOW, I'M NOT SAYING THERE'S ANYTHING *WRONG* WITH HAVING A JOB.

I WAS ABOUT TO *SAY*...

EVERYONE NEEDS SOME WAY OF GETTING STARTED, AND A JOB IS ONE WAY TO MAKE MONEY AND A GREAT WAY TO LEARN ABOUT A FIELD THAT INTERESTS YOU.

BUT THAT JOB'S NOT GONNA MAKE YOU RICH. IT'S THE THINGS THAT YOU *DO*, LIKE BUYING ASSETS AND NOT RACKING UP A BUNCH OF CREDIT CARD BILLS, THAT'LL MAKE YOU *RICH*.

51

52

5

Let's Do It!

55

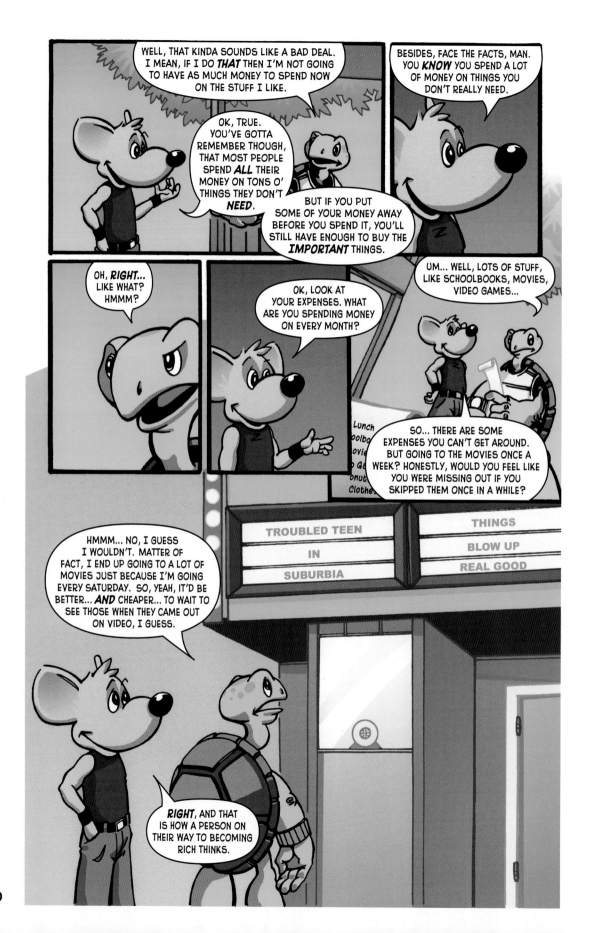

57

58

59

60

61

FOR INSTANCE, WHEN MOST PEOPLE WANT SOMETHING THEY USUALLY JUST GO OUT AND BUY IT. AND A LOT OF TIMES, WHEN THEY DON'T HAVE ENOUGH CASH THEY PUT IT ON CREDIT CARDS.

BUT THAT'S NOT THINKING THE WAY YOU HAVE TO IF YOU WANT TO BE RICH. ALL THAT LEAVES YOU WITH IS THE STUFF YOU WANTED BADLY AT THAT MOMENT— AND *NO* MONEY.

THAT STUFF'LL BREAK OR WEAR OUT OVER TIME AND THEN COST YOU *MORE* MONEY TO GET NEW STUFF TO REPLACE IT. THAT'S THE THING: IT *COSTS* YOU MONEY, INSTEAD OF *GIVING* YOU MONEY.

LOOK AT HOW THE RICH DO IT.

INSTEAD OF JUST RUNNING OUT AND BUYING WHAT THEY WANT, THEY USE THAT MONEY TO BUILD ASSETS INSTEAD.

THEN THEY MAKE THE ASSET GROW AND USE ITS PROFITS TO BUY WHATEVER IT WAS THEY WANTED.

BY INVESTING IN ASSETS, YOU ALWAYS HAVE CASH COMING AT YOU, TO SPEND HOWEVER YOU WANT, ALL WITHOUT WORKING AT A JOB.

66

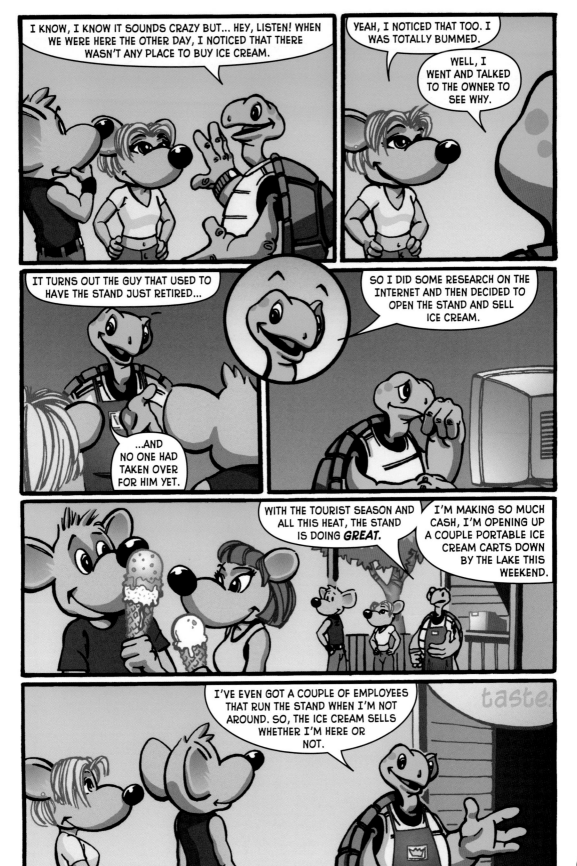

67

68

69

70

About the Author
Robert Kiyosaki

Best known as the author of *Rich Dad Poor Dad*—the #1 personal finance book of all time—Robert Kiyosaki has challenged and changed the way tens of millions of people around the world think about money. He is an entrepreneur, educator, and investor who believes the world needs more entrepreneurs who will create jobs.

With perspectives on money and investing that often contradict conventional wisdom, Robert has earned an international reputation for straight talk, irreverence, and courage and has become a passionate and outspoken advocate for financial education.

Robert and Kim Kiyosaki are founders of The Rich Dad Company, a financial education company, and creators of the *CASHFLOW*® games. In 2013, the company will leverage the global success of the Rich Dad games in the launch of a new and breakthrough offering in mobile and online gaming.

Robert has been heralded as a visionary who has a gift for simplifying complex concepts—ideas related to money, investing, finance, and economics—and has shared his personal journey to financial freedom in ways that resonate with audiences of all ages and backgrounds. His core principles and messages—like "your house is not an asset" and "invest for cash flow" and "savers are losers"—have ignited a firestorm of criticism and ridicule… only to have played out on the world economic stage over the past decade in ways that were both unsettling and prophetic.

His point of view is that "old" advice—go to college, get a good job, save money, get out of debt, invest for the long term, and diversify—has become obsolete advice in today's fast-paced Information Age. His Rich Dad philosophies and messages challenge the status quo. His teachings encourage people to become financially educated and to take an active role in investing for their future.

The author of 19 books, including the international blockbuster *Rich Dad Poor Dad*, Robert has been a featured guest with media outlets in every corner of the world—from CNN, the BBC, Fox News, Al Jazeera, GBTV and PBS, to *Larry King Live, Oprah, Peoples Daily, Sydney Morning Herald, The Doctors, Straits Times, Bloomberg, NPR, USA TODAY,* and hundreds of others—and his books have topped international bestsellers lists for more than a decade. He continues to teach and inspire audiences around the world.

His most recent books include *Unfair Advantage: What Schools Will Never Teach You About Money* and *Midas Touch*, the second book he has co-authored with Donald Trump. Robert's newest book, *Why "A" Students Work for "C" Students,* will be released in April of 2013.

To learn more, visit RichDad.com

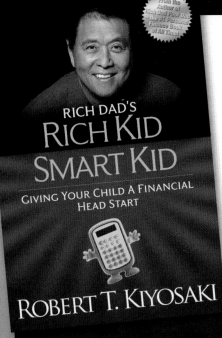

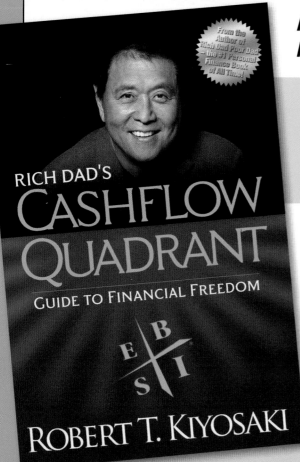

Rich Dad's Wisdom: The Power of Words

To improve your brain's financial power, improve your financial vocabulary. Words are fuel for your brain!

If you improve your financial vocabulary, you will become richer and richer. The good news is that words are free. It does not take money to make money.

Here is an example of the power of words:

Asset - Anything that puts money into your pocket whether or not you work.

Liability - Anything that takes money out of your pocket.

Expand your vocabulary by learning the financial terms in the glossary on the Rich Dad website (**richdad.com**) or get a dictionary of financial terms. As you look up financial words on a regular basis (or look up the definition of a term you hear but do not understand), you may find yourself becoming richer and richer.